Pages marked with ⬇ have a related downloadable free activity sheet at www.franklinwatts/downloads. Find out more on page 32.

Words in **bold** are in the glossary on page 30.

Before you start

These simple rules will make sure you stay safe when you cook:

- Wash your hands before and after preparing food.
- Ask an adult to help when the recipe uses the cooker or grill.
- If you have long hair, clip or tie it back.
- Dry your hands before you plug in or unplug any electrical appliances.
- Wear an apron or an old shirt.
- Wash up as you go along.
- Be extra careful with sharp knives.
- Ask an adult to help with the liquidiser/food processor.
- Ask an adult to help you weigh the ingredients.

Look out for this useful guide to each recipe.

How long each recipe takes to make.

How difficult each recipe is to make.

If the recipe needs to be cooked.

All about lunch

By lunchtime your body has used up the food you ate for breakfast. Lunch refuels your body until it is time for supper.

Hot or cold

Not everyone eats a hot meal at lunchtime. For a lot of people, lunch is a selection of cold foods packed at home and taken to school or work in a lunchbox. Cold food can be just as tasty as a hot meal - and just as good for you, too.

Fruit and vegetables

You should eat at least five portions of fruit and vegetables every day (5-a-day). They should make up about one-third of what you eat. Frozen, canned and dried fruits and vegetables all count. Try to eat lots of different coloured fruits.

Meat, fish, chicken, eggs and beans

These foods contain **protein**. Cooked meat and fish make good sandwich fillings (pages 8-9). Try adding them to a salad (pages 12-15) to make a complete meal that will keep you going until suppertime.

Be prepared

If you take a packed lunch to school, prepare as much as you can in advance. All the recipes in this book can be made the day before you eat them and kept in the fridge overnight.

The soup on pages 18-19 can be reheated in a pan. Pour the hot soup into a

This family is enjoying a healthy lunch with a variety of different foods.

vacuum flask and you will have a delicious warming meal waiting for you at lunchtime.

New ideas

Planning, preparing and cooking great-tasting lunches for yourself, friends and family is great fun. You get to eat well, too!

Think of all the things you would like to make for lunch in the next week. Look through this book for some new ideas for recipes.

Make a shopping list of the things you need.

To eat a **balanced diet** try not to eat the same foods every day. There are so many lovely foods to choose from - try experimenting with some new tastes!

Go shopping

Many people eat bread at lunchtime. There are a lot of different types of bread to choose from. They have a wide range of tastes and textures. Next time you visit a supermarket see how many types you can find.

Wholemeal, **wholewheat** or **wholegrain** bread is made from wholemeal flour that contains all of the **grain** including the brown outer layer called the **bran layer**. It contains lots of **vitamins**, **minerals** and **fibre**. As well as being good for you it also has lots of flavour.

White bread is made from wheat that has had the bran layer removed.

Pitta bread is a flat, oval bread which forms a pocket that can be filled.

This supermarket has a great variety of different types of bread to choose from.

Cheese and yoghurt

Cheese and yoghurt are convenient foods to take in a lunchbox.
- Look at the labels on yoghurts and choose the ones lowest in sugar and fat.

Starchy foods

You should eat **starchy** foods every day – they should make up about one third of what you eat. Examples include a portion of bread in sandwiches, or a rice or pasta salad.
- Choose wholegrain or wholewheat varieties.
- For a sweet alternative try the flapjacks (pages 26–27). They are made from oats which are another starchy food.

Labels

If you go shopping for food, look at the food labels. Some foods are very good for you. Foods that are high in salt, sugar or **fat** are bad for you if you eat them too often.

- Look for **low-salt**, **low-sugar** and **low-fat** foods (particularly if the fat is **saturated fat**) on food labels.

Supermarkets sell a wide range of foods made in handy sizes to put in lunchboxes. Many of these **processed foods** are high in sugar and fat. Some also have **artificial colourings** and **flavourings** to make them look more attractive. Eat them only very occasionally.

Chocolate bars and biscuits are full of sugar. Take a fruity pot (see pages 22–23) or take some fresh fruit instead.

Water

You need water for your body to perform well. You get some water from the foods you eat. You should drink six to eight glasses of water a day – more in hot weather.

Have more than one filling in these sandwiches for 'stacks' more taste and goodness.

You will need

Cream cheese and celery:
- sharp knife
- chopping board
- mixing bowl
- tablespoon
- kitchen knife

Chicken salad:
- sharp knife
- chopping board
- mixing bowl
- mixing spoon
- kitchen knife

Ingredients

- 3 small slices of bread – 2 brown and 1 white
- small amount of butter
- 2 different fillings
  Cream cheese and celery
- 1 stick celery
- 1 tablespoon cream cheese
  Chicken salad
- 1 piece cooked chicken (chopped)
- cucumber (chopped)
- 1 torn-up lettuce leaf

For more ideas for fillings see pages 10–11.

Prepare the fillings

Cream cheese and celery
- Slice the celery (see page 29).

- In a bowl, mix with a tablespoonful of cream cheese.

Chicken salad
- In a bowl, mix the chicken, cucumber and lettuce together.

- Butter both sides of the slice of white bread with the kitchen knife.
- Butter one side of each of the slices of brown bread.

- Place one slice of brown bread, butter-side up, on the chopping board.
- Spread the first filling on top.

- Put the white slice of bread on top of that.
- Cover with the second filling.

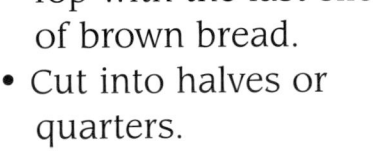

- Top with the last slice of brown bread.
- Cut into halves or quarters.

Tasty!

15 minutes

Easy

No cooking

Fishy pittas

Pitta breads are oval-shaped, flat breads. They make a perfect pocket to stuff with your favourite filling.

Ingredients

- small tin tuna fish in water or sunflower oil (drained)
- 1 tablespoon mayonnaise
- 1 large or 2 small pitta breads
- small amount of butter
- some shredded lettuce
- sliced tomato

You will need

- bowl
- fork
- tablespoon
- sharp knife
- kitchen knife
- plate

Fish
Fish is a good source of protein, vitamins and minerals. You should try to eat a portion of fish at least twice a week.

1

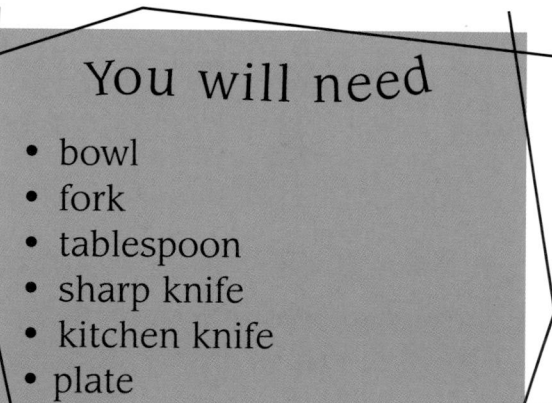

- Put the tuna fish into a bowl.
- Break it up with a fork.
- Add a tablespoon of mayonnaise and mix together.

2

- With a sharp knife, make a small cut in the side of the pitta bread. Open it up to make a pocket.

3

- Spread a little butter inside.

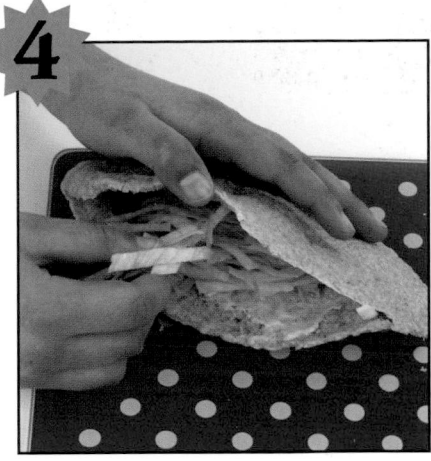

4

- Put the shredded lettuce into the bottom of the pocket.

5

- Put the tomato slices on top of the lettuce.

6

- Put spoonfuls of the filling on top of the lettuce and tomato.

Handy hint

Tinned salmon, smoked mackerel or cooked fresh salmon or tuna will all work well as fishy fillings for your pitta bread.

Lovely!

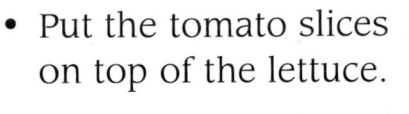

15 minutes

Easy

No cooking

Ri_ _alud

Try this colourful chicken and rice salad instead of a sandwich at lunchtime. It is easy to pack into a pot in your lunchbox.

Ingredients

- 100 g (3½ oz) brown rice
- 2 tablespoons of any of the following: sweetcorn, chopped red pepper (see page 28), leftover cooked green beans or peas
- 2 tablespoons chopped chicken
- 2 dessertspoons olive oil

This is enough for two portions.

Rice

Rice is a starchy food (see page 7). It gives you energy. Unlike white rice, brown rice has not had the outer bran layer removed. This means that as well as having more flavour, brown rice contains more vitamins, minerals and fibre than white rice.

You will need

- a small saucepan
- measuring jug
- colander
- mixing bowl
- dessertspoon

1

- Put the rice into the saucepan.
- Cover it with water.
- Put the saucepan on the hob and turn the hob on to high.

2

- When the water is **boiling**, turn the heat down to medium. Cook for the time given on the packet.
- Drain the rice in a colander placed in the sink.
- * Remember to turn the hob off.

- Put the drained rice into a bowl and leave to cool.
- When the rice is cool, add all the other ingredients.

- Mix everything together.
- Put a portion into a bowl.

- If you are taking the salad in your lunchbox, pack it in a plastic box with a lid. Remember to include a fork!

Mmm!

Cool it!

Fill a small plastic bottle with water, leaving a gap at the top. Place it in the freezer overnight. In the morning, put it into a plastic bag in your lunchbox. By lunchtime you will have a cold drink – and your food will be cool too.

| 40 minutes |
| Medium |
| Cooked |

Grapes
Cut in half

What you put in a salad bowl is up to you. Choose from the ingredients below and make up your own favourite salad.

Bottom layer
Choose from:

Tomato
Sliced

Sweetcorn

Cucumber
Chopped

Lettuce
Shredded

Pepper
Chopped

Celery
Sliced

Spring onions
Sliced

Top layer
Choose from:

Chicken
Chopped into chunks

Prawns

Hard-boiled egg
Sliced

Ham
Cut into strips

Tuna fish
Flaked

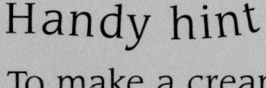

Cheese
Cubed or grated (see page 29).

Beautiful!

Handy hint
To make a creamy salad dressing, mix a tablespoon of creme fraiche with a few chopped chives and a squirt of lemon juice.

Handy hint
A few pumpkin or sunflower seeds sprinkled on a salad will add some extra crunch!

30 minutes

Easy

No cooking

15

Tortilla wrap

Tortilla wraps are available in supermarkets. They are a good way to wrap up your favourite filling for lunch.

Ingredients

- 1 tortilla
- 2 tablespoons cream cheese or creme fraiche
- cucumber slices (see page 29)
- tomato slices
- 1 dessertspoon hummus

Pulses

Pulses are a starchy food that also contain fibre and protein. They are a good source of protein for people who do not eat meat. Three heaped tablespoons of pulses also count as one of your 5-a-day (see page 4).
Hummus is made from pulses called chickpeas. It can be bought in supermarkets. Some varieties are high in fat and salt, so check the label.

1

- Spread the cream cheese or creme fraiche over the middle of the tortilla.

2

- Add a layer of cucumber slices.

3

- Add a layer of tomato slices.

• Add a dessertspoon of hummus.

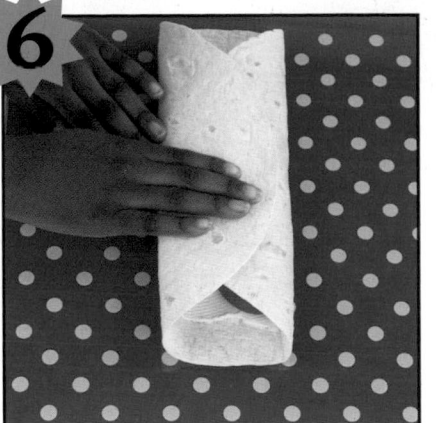

• Fold in one edge of the tortilla as shown above.

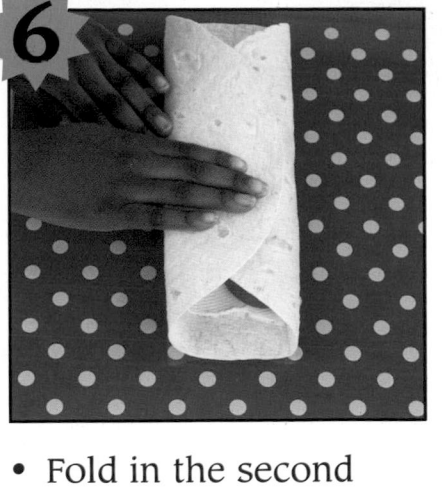

• Fold in the second edge as shown above.

• Fold the top down to the middle.

• Cut into two pieces diagonally.

Y u m m y !

• Turn and fold the bottom to the middle.

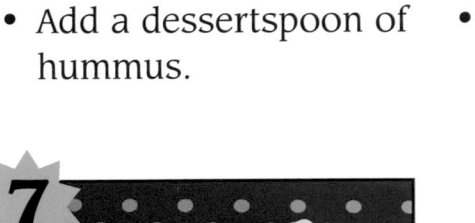

| 15 minutes |
| Easy |
| No cooking |

Vegetable soup

This velvety-smooth soup is easy to make and full of tasty vegetables.

1

- Peel and chop the onion (see page 28).

2

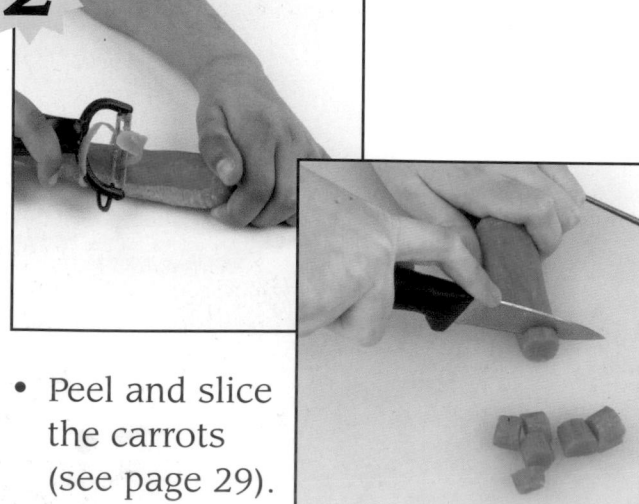

- Peel and slice the carrots (see page 29).

3

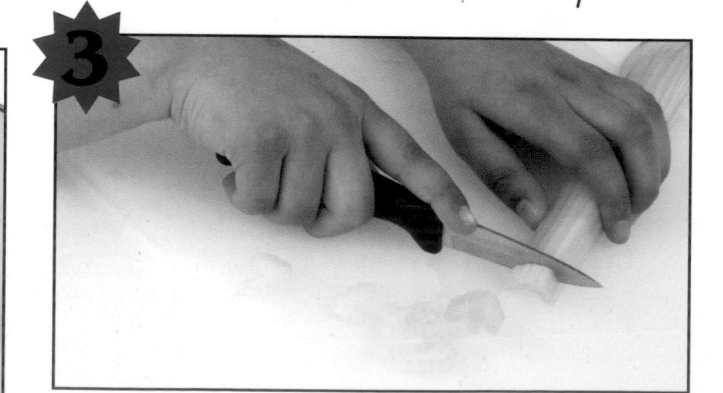

- Slice the stick of celery.

4

- Turn the hob on to a medium heat.
- Put the oil into the pan. Add the vegetables.
- Turn the heat down to low and keep stirring for 5 minutes.

- Pour the soup back into the pan and heat until almost boiling.
- * Remember to turn the hob off.

- Serve with a thick slice of wholemeal bread.

5

- Add the stock to the vegetables in the pan.
- Cook for 15-20 minutes, or until the vegetables are soft.

6

- Put the stock and cooked vegetables into a liquidiser and whizz until the mixture is smooth.

Vegelicious!

30 minutes
Medium
Cooked

Omelette slices

This thick Spanish-style omelette is delicious hot or cold. Serve it hot for a main meal and leave a couple of slices in the fridge for your lunchbox.

Ingredients

- 2 medium potatoes
- 1 tablespoon oil
- 1 onion (chopped see page 28)
- 3 eggs
- few strips red pepper (optional)

You will need

- peeler
- sharp knife
- chopping board
- heatproof frying pan
- fish slice
- small bowl and fork

1

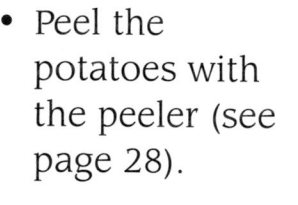

- Peel the potatoes with the peeler (see page 28).

2

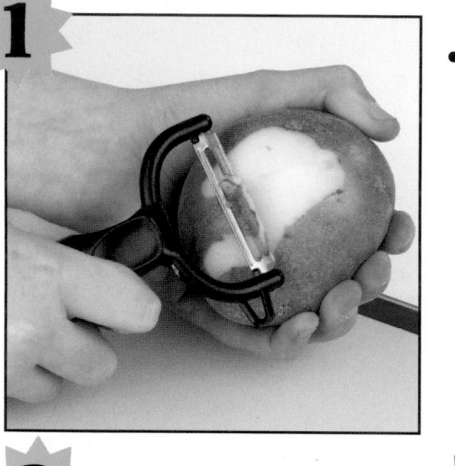

- Cut the potatoes into slices.
- Cut the slices into sticks and then into cubes (see page 28).

3

- Put the oil in the frying pan. Place the pan on the hob on a medium heat.
- Put the chopped onion, and potato cubes in the pan. Add the red pepper if you are including it.

4

- Leave them to cook for about 15 minutes, or until the potatoes break up easily when you press them with the fish slice.

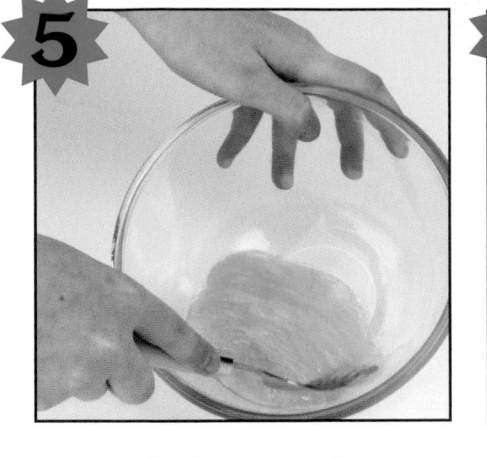

- Crack the eggs into a bowl (see page 29).
- Mix well with a fork.

- Tip the beaten eggs on top of the cooked potatoes and onions.
- Cook over a low heat for 10 minutes.

- Flip the omelette over with a fish slice (ask an adult to help).
- Cook for another minute.
* Remember to turn the hob off.

- Slide the omelette on to a plate.
- Cut into slices and enjoy it hot, or leave to cool.

Eggytastic!

Handy hint

If you have any leftover vegetables – such as onions or courgettes – you could chop them up and add them to the potato and onion.

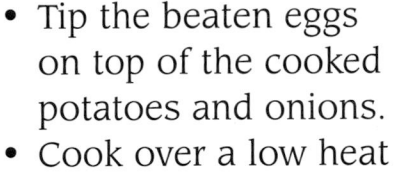

30 minutes

Tricky!

Cooked

Fruity pots

Fruity pots can be made using any fruits that you have available. Use some more unusual tropical fruits, or mix lots of different colours.

You will need

- small sharp knife
- bowl
- 4 glasses or a serving bowl
- measuring jug
- dessertspoon

Ingredients

- 4 leaves **gelatine**
- 225 g (8 oz) strawberries and raspberries washed and cut into pieces
- 50 ml (2 fl oz) boiling water
- 500 ml (18 fl oz) cranberry, grape or raspberry juice

If you prefer

To make a tropical pot, use orange segments, mango and pineapple (tinned, not fresh) with apple juice.

For a 'tutti-frutti' pot, use as many different-coloured fruits as you can, and top it up with white grape juice.

1

- Put the gelatine leaves into a bowl of cold water for a few minutes until they are soft.

2

- Divide the fruit pieces amongst the four glasses, or put them in the serving bowl.

3

- Put the softened gelatine into a measuring jug. Pour the measured boiling water over it.

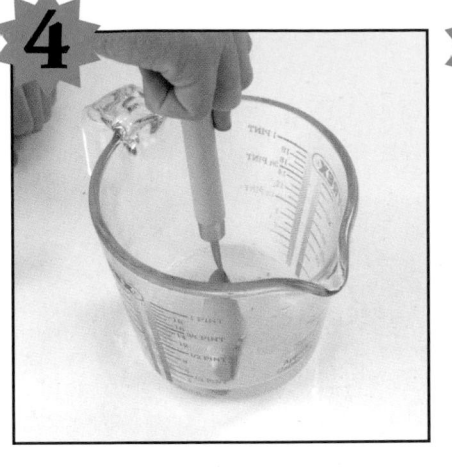

4

- Stir until the gelatine has melted into the water.

5

- Pour the fruit juice into the jug and stir to make a fruit jelly mixture.

6

- Pour the jelly over the fruit in the glasses or serving bowl.
- Leave to set in the fridge for a couple of hours.

More about 5-a-day

It is recommended that you eat at least five 80 g (3 oz) portions of fruit and vegetables every day. A portion is:

- One large fruit such as an apple, banana, orange or pear.
- One slice of a very large fruit, such as a melon or pineapple.
- A handful of dried fruit or small fruits such as cherries, strawberries or grapes.

Tinned and frozen fruits count too.

- If you are putting a jelly pot into a lunchbox, make it in a plastic pot that has a lid. To keep it cool, see the 'Handy hint' on page 13.

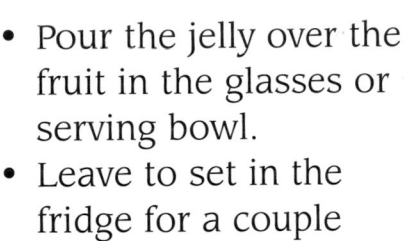

Wow!

20 minutes

Easy

No cooking

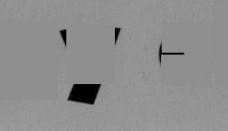

These delicious sweet treats are very easy to make. By adding the dried fruit they can also be one of your 5-a-day. They are perfect as a lunchbox treat.

You will need

- saucepan and a bowl that fits on the top of the saucepan
- wooden spoon
- 12 cake cases
- teaspoon

Ingredients

- 225 g (8 oz) chocolate
- 300 ml (10 fl oz) water
- 115 g (4 oz) rice crispies or cornflakes
- 55 g (2 oz) dried fruits such as raisins, glacé cherries or dried cranberries, coconut or chopped nuts

1
- Break the chocolate up into pieces and put the pieces in the bowl.

2
- Put the water into the saucepan and place the pan on the hob. Turn the hob on to a medium heat.

3
- Place the bowl on top of the saucepan. Stir the chocolate with a wooden spoon until it melts.
* Remember to turn the hob off.

- Take the bowl off the pan.
- Mix in the cereal and dried fruit.

- Spoon the mixture into the cake cases.
- Leave the cakes to cool in the fridge.

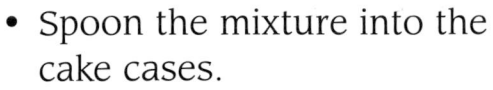

Scrummy

| 30 minutes |
| Medium |
| Cooked |

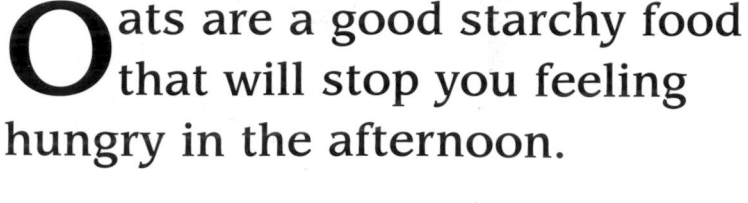
Oats are a good starchy food that will stop you feeling hungry in the afternoon.

Before you start

• Turn the oven on to 180°C (350°F).

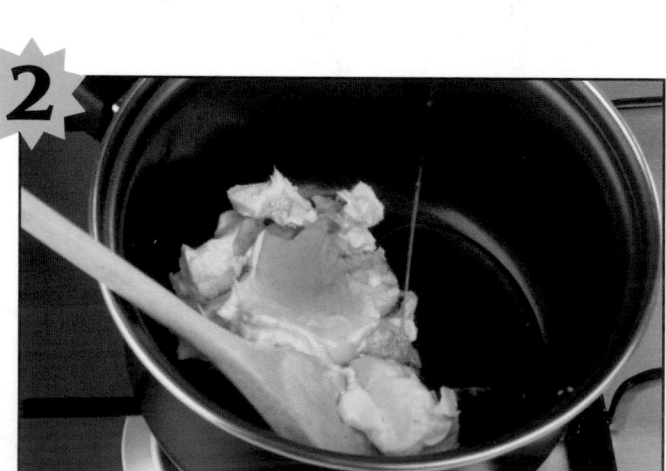

1

• Put the butter into the saucepan.

2

• Add the golden syrup and brown sugar.
• Turn the hob on to low.

3

• Heat the butter, syrup and sugar until they have melted.
* Remember to turn the hob off.
• Add the oats to the saucepan and stir them in with the wooden spoon.

4

• Tip the mixture into the tin.

5

• Smooth out with a kitchen knife.
• Bake in the preheated oven for 30 minutes.

6

• Take out of the oven and place the tin on the wire cooling rack.
• Cut into squares.
• Take the oat flapjacks out of the tin when they are cold.

Sweeeeet!

| 1 hour |
| Medium |
| Cooked |

How to!

Peel

To peel means to take off a small amount of the outside or skin of a fruit or vegetable.

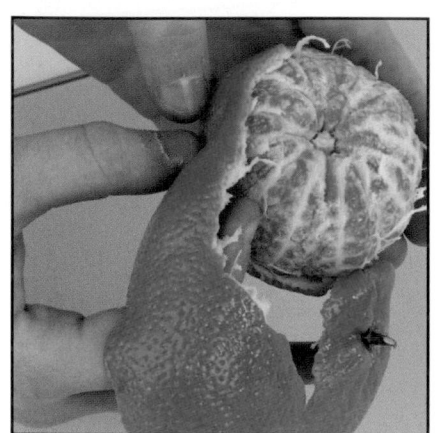

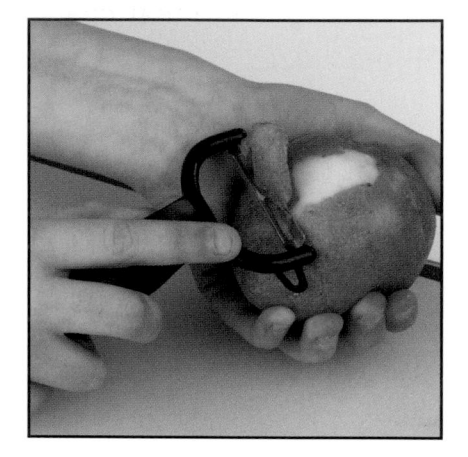

- Oranges have a thick peel. It is quite easy to take off with your fingers.

- To take the peel off potatoes, carrots or kiwi fruits, it is safer to use a peeler than a knife.

Chop

Chopping is cutting something into lots of equal-sized pieces. How small the pieces are depends on what you are cooking. Nuts, fruits, vegetables and meat can all be chopped.

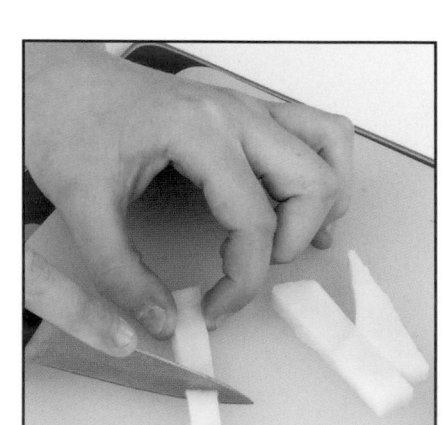

- Some things such as nuts need to be chopped very finely. You can do this in a food processor or liquidiser.

- To chop into larger chunks called cubes, first take off a thick slice. Cut the slice into pieces first one way, and then the other.

Slice

Slicing is preparing something by cutting a thin piece from it. Bread, cheese, cucumber, tomatoes, fruits, vegetables and meat can all be sliced.

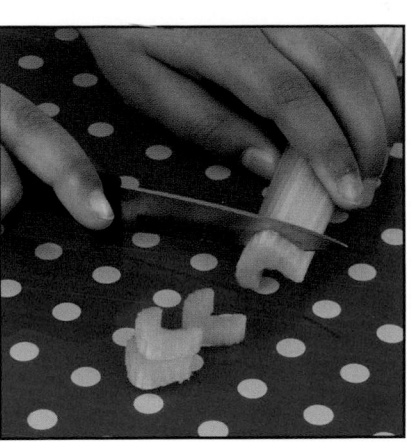

- Hold the food firmly. Do not hold too close to the end you are cutting.
- Cut across the food using a sawing action.

Grate

A food grater has lots of sharp blades that can turn food into strips.

A box grater has different-sized blades for different foods.

Cheese and carrots are best grated on the coarsest blades.

- Press the food against the blades and push down.

Crack open an egg

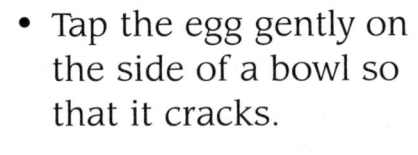

1

- Tap the egg gently on the side of a bowl so that it cracks.

2

- Put your thumbs on either side of the crack.

3

- Hold the egg over the bowl and gently pull the shell apart.

Glossary

artificial colouring Man-made colouring added to food.

artificial flavouring Man-made flavours added to food.

balanced diet A diet that contains all the foods necessary to grow and stay healthy.

boiling The point when a liquid becomes hot enough to make large bubbles that rise to the surface and break.

bran layer The hard outer layer of grain. It contains fibre, vitamins and minerals.

fat A greasy substance found in food. Fats are divided into two types: **saturated fats** are found in cream, cheese, butter, suet, lard, fatty meat and chocolate; **unsaturated fats** are found in avocados, nuts, vegetable oils and olive oils. Unsaturated fats are healthier than saturated fats.

fibre The part of a fruit or vegetable that cannot be digested. Fibre helps other food to be digested.

gelatine A setting agent used to make jellies and mousses. It is available as a powder or in sheets. Some gelatine is suitable for vegetarians. Check the label on the packet.

grain The starch seed of a plant such as wheat, corn, oats or rice.

low-fat Describes a food that does not contain a lot of fat.

low-salt Describes a food that does not contain a lot of salt.

low-sugar Describes a food that does not contain a lot of sugar.

mineral A substance such as iron or calcium that the body needs to function properly. Minerals are found in foods.

pitta bread A flat, oval bread which forms a pocket that can be filled.

processed food Any food product that has been changed in some way. Cooking, freezing, drying, canning and preserving are all methods of processing food. Processed foods may contain colourings, flavourings and other additives and preservatives.

protein A substance found in some foods. It is needed by the body to grow and develop properly. Meat, eggs, milk and some types of beans contain protein.

pulse A type of edible seed. Peas, beans and lentils are all pulses.

starchy Describes a food containing starch. Starchy foods make up one of the food groups. They include foods such as bread, cereals, rice, pasta and potatoes.

vacuum flask A flask that has double walls, used for keeping liquids hot or cold.

vitamin One of the substances that are essential in very small amounts in the body for normal growth and activity.

wholegrain Describes cereals such as wheat, barley and oats that have not had the outer layer taken off.

wholemeal Made from wholegrain flour.

wholewheat The entire grain of wheat, which includes the outer layer (bran).

Equipment

non-stick baking tray

cake cases

mixing bowl

wire cooling rack

measuring jug

fish slice

grater

chopping board

mixing spoon

whisk

tablespoon

dessertspoon

teaspoon

sharp knife

saucepan

colander

kitchen knife

frying pan

wooden spoons

You will also need:
  T-towel
  weighing scales
  oven glove

peeler

liquidiser

food processor

Index

Activity sheets

The following pages have accompanying sheets, which are available to download for free at www.franklinwatts.co.uk.

Pages 4–7 All about lunch
Plan your lunches for the week ahead on this handy food chart. Fill in the shopping list so you know what you need to buy.

Pages 8–9 Sandwich stacks
What sandwich fillings do your friends like best? Fill in this food survey to find out which are the most popular.

Page 31 Equipment
Download a colourful poster of all the equipment used in the 'Plan Prepare Cook' books.